NECROPOLE

A Meditation on Loneliness

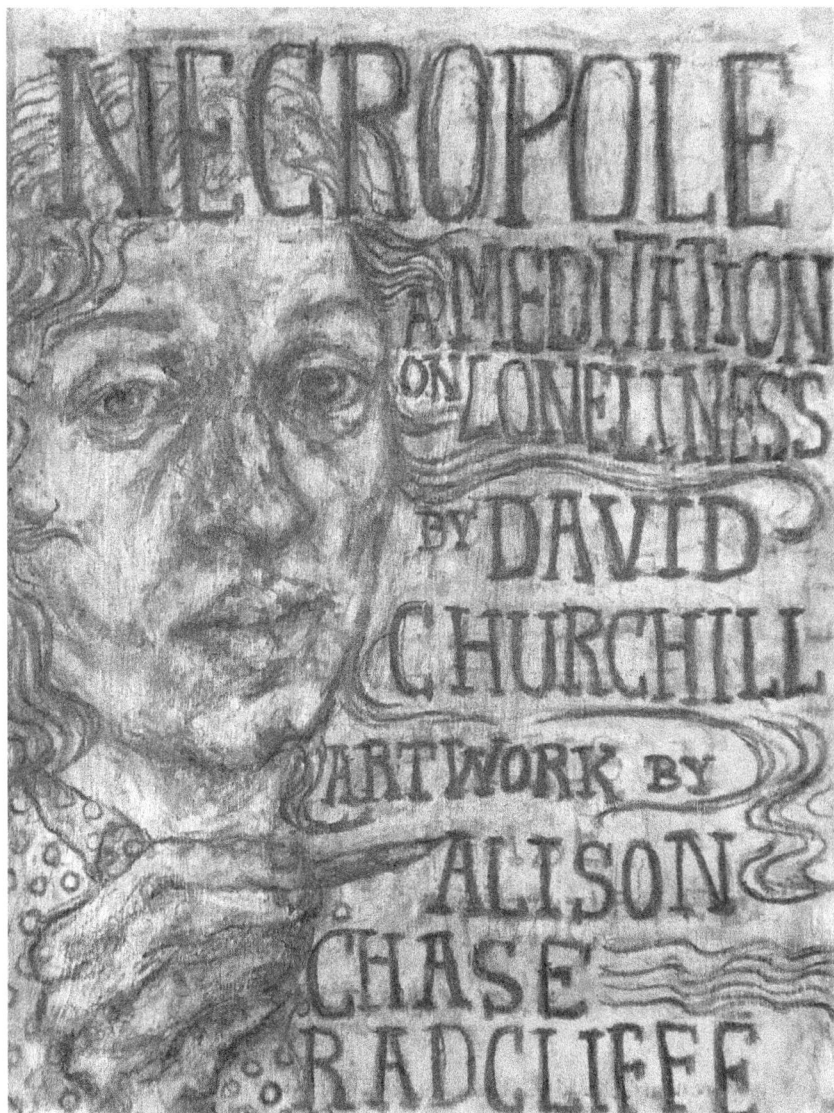

NECROPOLE

A MEDITATION ON LONELINESS

BY DAVID CHURCHILL

ARTWORK BY ALISON CHASE RADCLIFFE

NECROPOLE

© 2020, 2022 David Churchill
Interior Artwork © Alison Chase Radcliffe

Cover art: Mari Dein at Dreamstime.com
Interior artwork: Alison Chase Radcliffe
Book layout: Barbara Shaw

ISBN 978-0-9753095-6-8

Second Edition

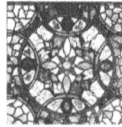

Published by:
Pony One Dog Press
Suite 113
1613 Harvard Street, NW
Washington, DC 20009

CONTENTS

PART ONE
The City

*Have you made yourself
what you seek,
a personal or philosopher's truth . . . ?*

I HAVE slipped
in the swift-falling snow,
running down through the
snow-covered cars
toward the still park
and the slow stream
and the thick boughs
bearing their trays of snow
and a pristine path
that belongs to me alone,

but today I don't slip—
I warm slowly
in a morning that seems
to awake with eyelids
that shred in their struggle
to rise,
as if refusing to rise,
or renew its blanket
a waking world will shed,
answering a call
nothing else shares . . .

Others who work rise early and run,
we are a crowd—
We share a silent world,
each alone in his own
breath—

headlights cutting gems
in the snow-shawl
along the path:

it is all we hear,
the breathing as we pass,
as though at that moment
we double-breathed,
the closest two
bodies can come—
Then alone again
with only one breath . . .

And how alone we are,
after we pass—
Disappearing into the snow
and a cloud
of our own physicality,
as though even bodies know
there should be more
between bodies
than breathing,
and a sudden fear comes:

we might never know
the moments when
it is enough,
because sometimes it is . . .

IF BODIES have spirits
workplaces have them too,
and this space that makes
a pretense of air,
a square fishbowl,
this office,

where air is conspicuous,
has the spirit
of an abandoned place,
a shuttered factory
where weeds line up
at outside doors
and cobwebs throng
and a cold calculation lives:
a soul in exchange
for a body.

David Churchill

The woman who waters
the ferns—
Her desk is decorated
with drawings by children.
She is the woman
who cleans the coffee-pot,
puts up the wreaths
and lays them away again.

Tomorrow her log-in
will fail, and when
she returns to her desk
the last time,
a silence will stall
on the cubicles around her.

One friend will follow
to the refuge of the restroom,
and a final Niagara
will signal the end of her.

I HAVE SPENT weeks
without working,
staring through the walls
at how the sky
sometimes reflects the city
that lies underneath it,
and sometimes its opposite,

as where the river flows,
above it a current
of slush over penguin commuters
falling over curbs,
and inverted snowbanks
already dirty,
and you almost see
lawn-chairs staking
claims to parking-places
in the cloud overhead . . .

My mind too reverses
over its thoughts,
and I'm suddenly under
the city before me,
among the herds speeding
through the dark
in the guts of worms.

Where worlds align,
a conveyor of stairway
taking people down
already in a dream-state,
and people coming up,
like lifts-full of miners
coming up from the depths . . .

I do not like these stairs.
I do not like people
who do not know
which direction they are going.

I do not like directions
that don't care.
I want a salvation with acrobats.

Yet while I day-dreamed
the clouds tore
like tissue
and the sun suddenly
like a slit-lamp
lit the snowbanks,
fixed a glory
in their ranks
and a flock of sparrows
at the ends of shadows.

Anyone still left
leaves now like a mole,
slowed in the rays
holding them back—
An unanswered phone
is a factory whistle.
Elevator chimes
sound a warning tone.

Some moments were made
only for one—
A spendthrift population
seems to have appointed
you
to be there for all of them.

The sunburst's last
lidded chamber
demands an answer
before it dies:
is God one or many?

THEN—a hurrying snow
like a late guest
obliges our happy-hour,
ushering with its sweep
each new arrival
into the lobby,
igniting every cheek's
alcoholic or brumal leaf—
People are glad
to be home
ahead of the storm;
we are in a lifeboat afloat
in a blizzard of stars,
glad of any disaster
for a reason to gather.

Yet I am outside,
filling with the downy fall
of an eternity in snow,
lost in the snow's statement
of infinite uniqueness,
each brief star rushing
to give itself up

in a union of stars
on the grave of the earth . . .

Or inside—propped
at the periphery of things,
against a pilaster
or under a sconce;
my gravity is off—
it repels instead of pulls.
You know, seeing me:
the ocean is too deep
to talk and tread water
that can drown you
in front of a life-guard.

To the children it is only
a wading-pool;
to dogs tethered
to controlling hands
it is always dry under foot.

I take refuge in memory . . .
Climbing the cushions
of mountains in houses
of strangers,
running through forests
of knee-caps and ankles . . .

A monkey on a frieze
in a Hindu temple,
—and a man kneeling

to school one sculpture
in indoor behavior.

Look around he says.
How many people
are here?

And you count and say
and he says no you
are missing one.

Again you count
and again you miss
one and
he counts and says see
there is one
more you can't see.

Then it happens.
A new dimension appears.
You step
out of the frieze.
You become free-standing.
You were the one
you couldn't see—
but now you see.

It takes hours for a body
to be birthed
but this is like missing
a step in the dark.

After that—everything
is a railing:
things that were made
to be stepping-stones,
sign-posts,
doorways without doors;
leaning on friends,
making lovers hold your hand.

You are that child
who now talks to himself.
You hear all your
own words twice.
You are checking
the thing you just said.
You repeat it to hear
if it passes some test,
according to a rulebook
you only just received,
but no time to read.

You are that child now
who monitors himself.
You no longer simply are;
You are under review.
You learn to review as you move;
you watch yourself living.
You will no longer utter
an unconsidered word.

And everywhere you looked then
you saw death:
you saw the cat
asleep at the curb
with bared teeth;
you saw a sparrow
resting its wings beneath a hedge—

You will become a young man
who clings to his dreams,
an old man who
having already
relinquished hearing and sight,
holds every doorframe,
every loss and rejection
on the way to the last door,
pushed by a world

that wants only one thing
for him,
to be as wise as his years,

but who does not ask what's next—
preferring the ignorance
of the young,
already gone
beyond a crumbling shore
that has lost its grip on the sea.

Those who do not stop
to join the glow
pass like sled-dogs
out of their traces,
bring the cold in
packed in their coats,
trot upward
to undomesticated kennels,

—too much in a hurry
to have a drink
with a neighbor:
the new people,
always arriving,
each in their own generation,
joining no tribe
but their own.

I watch them come in
and pass by.
Let them leave the snow
behind them,
the heavy sweep
and piling in the park,
street-light skirts
and piles on fences,
lone cars crawling
in covert lights—
Let them leave an old man in his shirt-sleeves . . .

Over left-overs
from the latest restaurants
they will open
slender devices
and read on glowing screens
TEN BRAIN HACKS
FOR A NEW YOU—
And while cheese
and crackers are cleared
away and uneaten snacks
carried back
to cranky apartments
from the lobby below,
new hands will rewrite
old lines,
new lives will seek
old wisdoms again . . .

TOWARD midnight snow
becomes sleet.
Handfuls of rice,
flung against windows,
as if somewhere in the night
forces were being joined;
in celebration,
I join images in my mind:

People on mats like
lily pads,
eyes tucked in their skulls,
the renovating generation,
the new people,

honest seekers in
painful groups
who will stumble onto
good ground
to frame questions on,

those who sit in circles
and make grudging
confession,
and strive to put space
between themselves
and their habits,

solitary saints of prayer and fasting
awakened to ecstasy—
Steel-clad youths

on chapel floors,
kneeling out the fires
of the body
while candles flicker down,

new age prophets
on wind-wrapped corners,
crying with voices
no one can hear:
Buddha is imminent—

And my mind cries STOP.
This will take you
where you should not go.

You are already
a child of successive
separations—
Take care you arrive
together with your end.

PART TWO
The Dead

COMES NOW a blind girl,
along the edge of the platform,
feeling with her stick.

I think I know why
the blind wear sunglasses,
though they can hardly
be blinded by any sun,

rather than blindfolds—
With too much the look
of the firing-squad,
that would unnerve us,
and those who are blind

dislike to unnerve
those they can't see.
So as I watch this girl
guiding through the crowd,
I try to imagine

what would it be like
to be in a world
of substance and sound
but no things,
not even the thing of blackness . . .

(Or do they see blackness,
nights without lights,
walls without light-switches?)

And if I could ask her
has she been blind
from birth,
and does she ever wonder
what she can't see,
like the aspect of things,

and what are these things
people call colors
no one can describe,
and if there are things
she can't even imagine?

As for us,
we have been given
a light that shows
two things only:
what we can eat
and what can eat us—
In a world of infinities,
are we not in this
someway like her?

For as at night when lovers embrace,
and something stirs
in the curtains
or breathes on their limbs,

as if their kiss had awakened
the future,
like a swarm of mayflies
on the shores of a lake
that waters the ages,

or as when an unremembered
dream returns
at mid-day,
or a sudden shiver
runs down the spine
in the middle of buying
a mackerel or shoe-strings,
are there not also
things we can't see?

And I would ask her,
if she could see again,
did she think we were blind too,
we who are day-blind,
can't see things
we've grown dull to seeing,
the daily world that
no longer aspires to sight . . .

LET HER FIND THE door of the car by herself.

David Churchill

Resist
the fellow-feeling of affection—
or impulse to help.
Do not touch without permission.

—Before you speak
the current sweeps
in and doors hit limbs—
she is standing before you
in a baggage of backpacks
and ear-buds
in a little space of her own.

24

I see the way the crowd
shifts around her,
neither seeing nor touching.
She holds her stick,
a scepter of the dead;
where she goes all are blind—

Suddenly I think could she
also be *lonely?*
Could someone have
given her a penalty
for being penalized,
a handicap for being handicapped,
if she lives alone?

Surely loving hands
must caress those cheeks,
dear lips kiss
those sightless eyes,
for no God could be so heartless . . .

—Or *is* loneliness God-given,
like ears too big
or a crooked nose?
Is it instead
a making of this world,
like a plague or paper-cut?

Still as if with a toss of defiance
she shakes her hair—

and generations of the lonely
dislodge
like droplets of rain.

I in a doorway
watch their free-fall,
feeling a pull that seems only
of the world,
a yearning that is only
a physical hunger,
like magnets yearning
for their opposite poles,
keys yearning for their locks,
snow yearning
for the blanket of the ground.

As if aware
of being watched
too long by one person,
she lifted the lenses
that shielded her eyes,
that turned back
blindness on eyes
made to see eyes,
toward me—
reflective in the subway glare,

and I saw myself
among them,
falling into dive-bars,
into corners of sports-bars,

a single figure
taking up whole tables
in coffee-house bars.

—I looked away then,
having seen enough.
I have paced out too much of my life
on oblivious sidewalks,
where around every corner
an empty apartment awaits,
a meal for one
in a paper bowl,
another unrestful sleep,
to want to endure more . . .

Do you sleep, girl without sun-rise?
Do you even know
when you are asleep?
Are you asleep now,
lulled by the rocking
of the train,
the gentle sway of its crowd?

Do you see in your sleep
what you can't see awake?
Do the invisible forms
of the day creep out
like the shy things they are,
when it's safe?

She touched her glasses—
as if to remove them,
reveal a slender face
askew about the eyes—
but didn't . . .

Instead as if to bring
some spectral feature into focus,
as if to brush
some cobweb from a factory door,
or see headlights cross
a darkened room—
she freed the delicate nose
beneath their steely hold,
shed a wrinkle
and set them back,

gesture of release for all
who like bat-flights
in the corner of an eye,
flee closing-time bars . . .

as only she can see them:
arms out in emptiness,
feeling a way through
fogs of breath-frost—
wondering who these
are they can't see,
sleeve-brush of nothings,
reflections whose sources
are more-distant reflections,

who that out-breath was,
that smoke that disappeared
when you asked of it
only a name . . .

They say ghosts too
drift like this
through immaterial worlds,
hands out in fingerless gloves,
yearning for touch . . .

—OR TELL ME, girl without sight,
do *we* make it,
this thing called loneliness,
like cars and railroad-ties
on factory floors,
on assembly-lines of loneliness,
or planned in the brains
of bureaucracy workers?

Doors opened and the car spewed
into a tatterdemalion multitude,
an ocean with no shore
and no center but
one multi-pointed destination,
flowing up and down
among different levels—

The blind girl picked
an unerring way,
while crowd-currents came,
pushing me aside—
I saw her diminish—
a dark diminishing flourish
of hair far ahead,
moving with a certainty
only the blind,
untroubled by crowds,
can achieve—
Every face that blocked me
cried to me FOLLOW HER, FOLLOW HER—

I wanted to help you,
to guide you,
feel your hand truthfully
in mine as I led you
to safety—
yet you are guiding me,
yet I am needing you.

What kind of mind
can move among crowds
without error—?
As though sight itself
was the hindrance,
blindness a kind of seeing?

I think consciousness is a space
to put things in,

a warehouse as big as the cosmos.
It holds things and ideas
of things,
feelings and thoughts
about feelings.
It holds the self
and versions of the self.
It holds hopes for the self.
It holds ennui and boredom,
and when the sun
crests in December,
a fluttering joy.
It holds other people.

I think consciousness
holds crates that were meant
to be delivered
but never arrived,
their labels tattered and unreadable.
Some spaces are like cities
where boarded-up houses decay
under dead street-lights;
others like libraries,
constructed by people
who like facts on a shelf,
and you can tell
which facts are thought often
and which never at all . . .

My space is a landfill
and parts are on fire—

David Churchill

Others like to go
to the edge of their space
and stand there alone,
staring into the darkness
beyond it.

I believe the space
of this blind girl
contains the streams of the crowd,
the where-from's
and where-to's
of each face in the crowd.
She knows which stream
leads to the next train . . .

As for me—the crowd
only confuses me.
I have no clue where we are.
The signs are out of order,
the conductor is announcing
stations in other cities.
I believe the blind girl
is traveling in a circle.
If I weren't following
I might know where we were.
We're on the same train
but I'm one car behind now.

Toward midnight
the crowds begin to thin.

Platforms grow cavernous
and begin to look
like ghost-towns.
I begin to be noticed.

Suddenly no one is asleep or
nodding-off anymore.
Glances grow hard,
chiseling a question:
why are you
following this woman?

I have no answer.
An emptiness
answers them back.
Perhaps there is a blind girl
in the heart of every man.
I need to go home . . .

NOW THE two of us
are alone in one car,
looking at each other
from opposite ends.
It takes all my nerve
to endure her dark stare.
As if she were sighted,
I find elsewhere to look.
I can't make eye-contact.

David Churchill

We're getting closer
to meeting as equals.

WHEN WE emerged,
riding up a stumbling
ladder toward the light
of low-lying stars,
bright empty store-fronts
broke in on me
along empty streets,
the night clear overhead,
but all the stars
were mixed up
and Orion was in bed—
One bar was open.

Indistinct or hunched
forms thickened the shadows
around a lamp
left on in a junk-shop;

Christmas lights above the bar
were a constellation
of defiance.
Some places on earth
are equalizers of men,
and this was one:
sight was no advantage here.

A drunk stumbled over
the blind girl's stick—
I wrote on a napkin
"I'll have what she's having."

A store was still open—
The strange bitter
drink dissolved
the junk-shop around me
and narrow aisles
stocked with dim items
took it's place;
the blind girl felt her way
along the soup cans
and cereal boxes—
and I followed quietly,
picking up the items
her fingers that were blind too
failed to replace.

She stopped—
Suddenly I was naked,
nowhere to hide.
She seemed to do a sum
in her head—
Then as if something
didn't add up,
with a hand like a paw
pushed another
box off the shelf—

I let it lie
until she rounded the corner,
bought a quick
pack of gum
and followed her out.

The city lay like a drunk
in an alley
amid a low glimmer
of sleeping snow,
one arm in the street;
discrepant store-fronts
were wrapped in a protective dark.
There was only
one house on the block.

The stick of the blind girl
cleared a path
toward its steps.

Was there any light on,
or were all the windows dark?

I stopped suddenly,
afraid to find out.
I wanted to believe
someone was waiting.
Too late I remembered:
do not touch without permission.
It was only for *me*,
this invasion of privacy.

Too late—

PART THREE
Eurydice

And when, abruptly,
the god stopped her
and said with sorrow:
He has turned around—
she could not understand,
and said softly Who?

—Rilke

WHY HAVE you followed me?

I can't see anyone—
Why is it possible
for anyone to see me?
I can't follow you—
Why is it fair
for you to follow me?
The whole world
is anonymous to me—
Do I not have
an equal right to anonymity?

You know nothing
about anything
I would want to know.
Why do you think
I know anything
you would want to know?

Let me follow you.
Lead me into your world.
Lead me into
that space where
everyone stands
with their backs to each other.

You have eyes and I,
a stick.
Shall we trade weapons?
Or may I see you,
yes, with my stick,
your head, your face, your eyes?
Let *go*! —You don't
want to be seen either.

You already know
about loneliness.
Your thoughts are loneliness.
Your mind
is a mind of loneliness.

Loneliness
has made you a stalker.

PART FOUR
Night

We are but skin about a wind . . .

—*Djuna Barnes*

SPRING WAS a long time coming
that year—
The snow drew back
slowly over its bones
and the bones shrank slowly
over concrete and brick
like glaciers giving up their dead:
rat tails and
cigarette butts
and plastic bags and condoms,
umbrellas and beach-chairs
and traffic cones
and unclaimed dog waste,
perishable and imperishable alike,
and gutters clogged
and trees never dried out enough
to bud and tires blew
and cars broke axles,
people turned ankles
on crumbling sidewalks

and ice lingered
on the shadowed stretches
of the run-path
and runners slipped
trying to avoid them,

and kept their eyes
to themselves
and ran in the mud,

and dogs rolled
in the mud
and owners looked for places
to wipe off their feet
and found none . . .

For others business picked up,
including for me,
not always an unwelcome
occurrence,
bringing with it more
need to travel
and less time to think,
hardly noticing
any change in the season
till after it changed,
then thinking how quickly it passed,
winter and all,
the days like laundry
slips or ticket stubs
scattered over an emerging resolve,
as a mood
slowly withdraws—

Visiting clients
and going to conferences.
I didn't miss the weather
at home.

The winter months
had been a night without sleep,
leaving me wondering
where I could get
what I needed,
that sleep had denied;

I walked an embankment
in one city
under the boughs
of recovering trees,
and felt I had been abandoned
by a condoling spirit;

and wondered
why it was so hard
to lose oneself
in over-heated meeting rooms,
or watching
vending-machine coffee
seep through a cup—

Sometimes I am not
proud of the job I do
but that spring
like a dead tree almost
glad to be free
of the load on its boughs,
I felt nothing at all,

David Churchill

putting dissatisfied employees
on committees
to decorate the office
or plan the next holiday party,
who already have
enough work to do—

Who don't really care
about holiday parties
or elevator music
made visible on their walls,
but lacked a name to
call what was really
wrong with their jobs,

who were being punished
for speaking the truth
and would know better
next time,
to keep their mouths shut.

I felt nothing, advising
employees to pick
a sister-department,
to job-shadow each other,
hold office-parties together,
to bring community
and friendship into the office,
knowing community
and friendship don't flow that direction,

but like a paper-towel
on a wet table,
anonymity and insignificance,
the awareness of being
as conscionable
as a gasket on a tractor,
seeps outward;
workers bring it home
like a pallor on their skin.

Yet after everyone had left,
pulled by the draining rays
to resurrect again
the who-they-are
in alternative settings,

despite the unfamiliar
floor-plan
I seemed to come into my own again,
a Caruso wandering
through offices of strangers,

testing once again
if an empty office after
closing time
is still preferable to a hotel room:

offices without pictures
for those who
embrace their anonymity,

others with pictures
of only themselves,
still others with walls
like the walls of dive restaurants,
making you wonder
if the lonely
really feel less alone
among their own kind . . .

An organizational plan
in one room
sprawled across three white-boards
and a wall,
where some wag had written
Department of the Universe,
Department of Humanity,
Department of Existence,
and down at a far corner
under an over-large arrow
at the edge of the frame,
a tiny stick-figure, *"You are here."*

I thought then of stick-figures
on cave walls,
then of the image of man choate
on a chapel ceiling . . .

I recalled a museum,
all the lofty galleries,
the stone figures
in their stages of beauty,

and the colorful panels
of mothers and babies
and ermined burghers
and their daughters,
and felt my sight
drawn to a focus,

then as if over-focused
dissolving again
among lily pads
and sheaves of wheat
and dappled picnics in the shade
and a woman descending
a staircase
in denuded motion—

Until only chaos remained,
kindergarten colors
and shapes without shapes,
and I thought
how did it come to this?
From a world of the senses,
feel of a body's
grain on stone,
fresh wind on pliant canvas,
to a world of ideas,
—and the image of Man is not here.

David Churchill

BUT SADDEST ARE the words
strangers speak
in the bars of hotels,
when the impersonality
of corporate surroundings,
aphrodisiac of hallways
and expense accounts
work their loosening on them,
to the honest music of slots
from adjoining rooms.

Worn-out scripts stick
like toffee to their gums again,
and inauthenticity
stiffens like a cleft-lip—

Though when they go to a room
they will no longer
be children
learning how to kiss
from lovers on a screen;
they will park their souls
and let their bodies take over;

in the morning
one will be glad
the other is leaving
and one will be sad
it won't lead any further—

Coins gush in a tray
and a part of you
wonders who won
and a part doesn't care.

The bar-back appears
with a chorus of glasses,
It is already late—
Whoever is still in the bar
at this hour
will sleep alone tonight,
but I am not alone.
My good friend Buddy Wiser
brought a few friends
to help cheer me up.

Might it almost be better
not even to seek friends?

But make open the place
where friends come instead,

perhaps the only
place friends *can* come from,
as if in some way
friends actually come from inside,
out of who we are—

Then slowly but increasingly
every bore-hole, sewer drain,
well, sink-hole, cenote and
blue-hole I had ever seen
merged in a bottomless
hole of all holes,

and somehow
without being seen
because it was already vast
this hole of all holes
continued to grow
and a wind blew out of it
and a personal cold
until it was a bottomless cavern,

and a band of pithecines
approached its lip,
threw one of their own
who no longer moved
into it,

and the first feeling
a human ever felt
no one would never forget
came out of it—

ONE THING about seasons:
they can't be stopped;
whether we notice or not
ice will lurch
into grass already needing
to be cut
and snow into downpours
that litter streets
with bloodless limbs
and make trees fall on cars;

and people feel forced
ahead and deprived
of their will,
who notice for the first time
there is nothing gentle
in new leaves,
or look with despair
on the cruelness
of crocuses in new snow—

Cafes set their tables out
too soon,
and people turn their collars up,
try to hold napkins down . . .

This is the season
that raises its dead inside us,
strews its questions
like petals over frozen ground—

Why don't we know
when the vulnerable
see us as a threat?

PART FIVE
Sleepwalk

*If I may tell a story, Simmias, about the things
on the earth that is below the heaven, and what
they are like, it is well worth hearing.*

—Socrates, PHAEDO

I'M THE PERSON who
set off alarms in museums.
I can't see anything
and that seems to scare them.

I love the feel of the high
cool air,
the sense of space molded
by interesting shapes,
domes and barrel-vaults,
the sound of words spoken
in shadow-type,
I love the ormolu of gilded
edges feeling me back;
I got caught with my tongue
on the glaze of a canvas once
when I thought I was alone . . .
—*That* wasn't easy to explain.
What's someone like you
doing in a place like this he said.
You'd be surprised I said;
In museums you feel free.

Here is a painting I saw.
Which museum or gallery
it hangs in I don't remember—
I remember *it*
and the rest is insignificant:

David Churchill

I will tell you what I saw.
I will use the clearest words
possible.

First off it's a landscape,
totally flat, all marsh and water;
I think it might be Dutch,
but there are no windmills—
Low swampy ground
surrounded by rivers and streams,
an estuary perhaps.

The thing is—it's totally black,
like night but darker than night,
no moon or stars;
you still know what's there
but you can't see anything;
people who were blind
where they came from,
get their sight back
when they come here,
so they can know what it's like
to be able to see
and not see anything . . .

And the scene is full of people—
I almost forgot that.
It wouldn't be anything
without the people:
crossing the water in different boats
and floating in the water,

crowding and huddled
on what ground there is
and wading in the marshes,
all coming and going
and standing around
and trying to get on firmer ground—

And the sound—!
I know it's just a painting
and sound is not a particular
quality of paint
but I'm telling you
this painting is that good!
The bubble and hum
of a multitude
and splash and sucking
of the muck and people
calling and cursing,

trying to find each other
and crying for help
and sorting themselves out
and trying to steady each other
and asking if anyone
knows what's going on,
but you have a suspicion
they already know . . .

But above all else
trying not to get pushed

into the water
in one particular direction,
one direction they can't see
but know in a dark
as black as squid ink—

Here's where the skill
of the painter comes into play.
He—or she—because
I don't remember who,
—the audio cut off—
succeeded in painting
something no one can see
because it exists underground:
out in the water,
where nobody wants to go
but already some people
are splashing and drifting
toward it, calling for help,
a beaded edge stitching
a sliver of not-light,
like a sink full of water
when it starts to flow over
in a bathroom at night;
there four rivers pour
into a bottomless cavern.

You'd think the roar
would drown everything
out—but it doesn't.
The buzz of the crowd

and individual cries,
all heard above or
almost in spite of
the thunder of a hundred
Niagara's and a Himalaya
of waves
booming in a bottomless sea-cave.

Nobody tells you but
somehow you know
most people will return
to where they're from,
after their allotted time,
but as much as they
forget everything else
after they get back,
they never get the roar
of those rivers
out of their ears,
or the thunder of the waves
in that bottomless cave . . .

SOMETIMES WHEN I'm not
in the mood for art,
I like to make a nuisance
of myself in a china shop,
or go to a store when a sale is on.

I can get away with things
most people can't—

and I wouldn't trade anything
for the ability to do it.
I'm just as insufferable

in person people say,
but sometimes I think
we who are helpless
are the only ones left
who can break any barriers.

The only people I want
for my friends are the few
who can put up with me.
They know who they are.
They leave everything behind
to put up with me.

Yet still my thoughts return
to the people in that painting,
who only stay for a time
then go back
where they came.
How do they pick up their lives
with the sound of that cave
in their hearts,
inside their hearts
where everything is dark,
their souls
like water circling a drain—?

The greatest danger for humans
is always the most real,
no matter how comfortable
or blessed is everything else;
always that one thing
outshadows everything.

Maybe they find themselves
holding onto each other,
shaking hands too long
when the other lets go,
hugging too hard then
feeling embarrassed . . .

Maybe others
don't want to be touched at all,
they have a feeling
of being pulled into danger,
don't want to be entangled
but don't know why—

Others hold onto their thoughts,
hold their feelings too tight,
as though in the space
of their souls these ideas
and feelings were the people
I saw in that painting,
lest something slip loose
and go down the drain,
any little part lost,
too much to lose . . .

Philosophers used to talk
about knowing things
before you were born
you could be taught to recall,
and maybe it's true,

and that would be good:
the worst is to not
have a name for that thing,
to not know what it is,
never knowing why your
heart starts racing
when the doors of the bus close

or your hands shake
when someone fills a tub,
and you think something
happened that's buried
in your mind,
and you try to remember,

while others don't want any
memories at all—
Who go out among friends,
live only for the moment
and drink till they pass out
and feel better
next morning, not remembering
the night before.

Sometimes I think
this will happen to me.
My eyes have already passed out.

I will be like some person
who's not even real,
whose only purpose
is to hand out tracts
on a corner,
you don't look at as you pass:

"Whoever would seek
an answer from life,
must stand alone
before existence
and ask it their question."

I will be the best
hander-outer of tracts
the world has ever seen.

PART SIX
Necropole

RANDOM PEOPLE ringing bells,
as if we had to be told
another year had passed,
and it was a reason
to celebrate something,
like a rebirth of spending,
stoked by carols;

new forests grow
in parking lots,
and an inflatable creche
springs a leak
in somebody's yard;

you almost want to dust the snow
from the sleeping
drunk outside
the liquor store—

It's the most complicated
time of the year;
so much has piled up,
it's like the attic
in an old woman's home.
One must return
to the beginning of things.

Begin with the early dark,
the dead flowerbeds,
to the ice
in the bird bath,
and the birds
that stay warm in flocks.

Some will not last the winter;
spring rains will
wash limp feathers
down thawing drains—

But I have heard them
in their numbers,
excited to be alive
in a sidewalk hedge,

when people cover their ears
in the morning frost,
and tighten scarves
around fragile throats—

They seem so one with the seasons,
they know nothing
of heat or frost,
only if the mood
is good, or bad,
and need no calendar to know it . . .

Their world is an armillary cage:
circles on circles,

how it is in part,
so it is in the whole.

Every sparrow is a world
in itself.
No sparrow is lonely,
not even the sparrow
that flies in the subway.
Every sparrow is a prophet.

There is a terrible
darkness in the heart
of each member of the flock,
but their clouds
do not conceal it,
their wings
declare it to the world.

They are at one
with their hedge,
with their scrummage of crumbs;
even alone they
are at one with themselves.

Not for us
the headlines of the times
their living
seems to say,
that gust about men's feet
where the homeless lie,

but the small print,
the writings
in the margins,
the little writings
of the world we throw away . . .

ARTWORK

Page 5: *Imaginary Friend 2*, pencil, pen, & oil on cardboard, 2015

Page 13: *Jamie*, 2018

Page 24: *Marcia* (crop) *from Marcia and Phil*, oil on cardboard, 2018

Page 35: *Omen (The Dog)*, oil on cardboard, 2018

Page 42: *Painter in a Bar*, charcoal & acrylic on cardboard, 2018

Page 53: *That Looks Like Me*, linoleum cut print on papger, 2016

Page 56: *Portrait of Ba*, charcoal & acrylic on masonite, 2019

Page 66: *I Don't Have Enough Feelings*, pencil & pen on paper, 2014

Page 68: *Mom, Reclining, Colorful Dark Room*, charcoal & oil on cardboard, 2019

Page 74: *Everlasting Dying Still Life*, pen on watercolor paper, 2020

ABOUT THE ARTIST

Alison Chase Radciffe is both an artist and musician. She grew up steeped in traditional music and surrounded by working artists. Her own drawings and paintings can be described as psychological portraiture. "Art and music are my tools to investigate and present a coherent expression of the universal experience of joy and sorrow. I approach the past and the present as one state of being, and seek answers with artifacts from my imagination as well as engaging social dialogue through portraiture." As a musician, she works in blues, spirituals, jazz, and soul. She also arranges and performs traditional music, as well as composes originals for vocals and keys.

Some of her more recent exhibitions and performances include the following:
"Welcome To The Rainbow Lodge" Solo Exhibition and Musical Performance by Alison Chase Radcliffe, Dorchester Center for the Arts, MD State Arts Council, Cambridge, MD
"Pictured People, Painted Faces" Exhibition of Portraits by Alison Chase Radcliffe, Jack Radcliffe, and Dave DeRan, Musical Performance by Alison Chase Radcliffe, The Liriodendron Mansion, Bel Air, MD
Oscar Marion Memorial, Musical Performance by Alison Chase Radcliffe, Arlington Cemetary

Her recordings include "Doris in Mind," "Songs of Peace and Forgiveness," "I Want Jesus to Walk with Me," "Soul of a People" Smithsonian Documentary Soundtrack, and her new EP "Hard Feelings."

A fuller list of her recordings and artwork, as well as upcoming Art/Music Shows, can be found on her website and on social media:
alisonchaseradcliffe.com
fb: facebook.com/alisonchaseradcliffe
ig: instagram.com/alison_radcliffe/